UNDERDEVELOPMENT, ECONOMIC DISTRESS, DISGRUNTLED HUMANITY, AND TERRORISM: IMPACTS OF 'EXTREMISM' IN NATIONS AS TALIBAN

VOLUME 1, ISSUE 4 OF BRILLOPEDIA

YATINDRA CHOUDHARY

ISBN 979-888521598-5

Contents

Preface

"Start writing, no matter what. The water does not flow until the faucet is turned on".

-Louis L'Amour

Hundreds of students and professors are contributing their work to Brillopedia, we are here to provide ample information about Law and Contemporary issues. Our aim is to provide a platform for today's generation to express their views and ideas on law and contemporary law.

Publication

This research paper is published in volume 1, issue 4 of Brillopedia

Author

Yatindra Choudhary

CHAPTER ONE

ABSTRACT

The Taliban swept into Afghanistan's capital after the government collapsed and the battered president joined an evacuation of his fellow citizens and foreigners. The article is an attempt to explore the reasons behind the dread caused by the name of nations like Taliban, most of which are 'Extremism' and 'Terrorism'. The state of economy (although having sufficient resources is not sustainable as a part of a healthy globe) and scope of development in Islamic nations like Taliban has been discussed followed by the consequences of misinterpreted 'Sharia law' on the humanity and a peace-enduring religion like Islam. The author has tried to bring into light the impacts of Sharia law and Radical Islam on women and Islamic society in general heading towards a discontented humanity. And while we are discussing Taliban and Terrorism, it becomes vital for us to understand the religious sources of Islam which are being misconstrued as of one acknowledging violence and obstructing progress of its disciples. The extremism/fanaticism/radicalism is a bigger threat to the world than any 'Religion'.

KEY WORDS: Taliban, Economy, Islam, Sharia, Women, Religion, Extremism, Terrorism.

CHAPTER TWO

INTRODUCTION

Ever since the economic rise of the West, the question of whether non-Western religions are ill-suited to economic efficiency and growth has attracted academic scrutiny. Special attention has been paid to the economic effects of *Islam*, the world's second largest religion after Christianity. Many negative claims are found in scholarly works. One reads, for instance, that Islam encourages in its followers' beliefs harmful to economic advancement. It is also said that *Islam* discourages human capital formation, limits experimentation and innovation, promotes hostility to commerce, and distorts markets by facilitating authoritarian governance. A very common view is that *Islam's* financial rules are incompatible with modern economic life.[1]

The Taliban might have seized Afghanistan, but a hefty task now lies ahead of them – managing a fragile and dependent economy and gaining access to the country's money. Even though they have dominated the political scenario of the country, they lack access to the billions of dollars that it has in reserves. The Afghanistan economy they have inherited this time is much more urbanised and almost tripled in size since they were last in power about 2 decades ago. However, economic challenges remain.[2]

While the Afghan Taliban have delivered numerous detailed critiques of the post-2001 order, they have publicly offered few alternatives. Beyond vague references to *Sharia* law and a state 'independent' of foreign domination, the Taliban's vision for the shape of the state after the withdrawal of foreign troops is, at least in public, quite ambiguous. The movements' obsession with the ongoing fight against the Afghan government and its international supporters has meant that questions about the future posed to Taliban leaders have resulted in evasive or imprecise answers. For example, in a 2009 interview Mullah Beradar, then the movements' deputy leader, referenced the possibility of talks and the shape of a post-withdrawal government with a concise reply: "This will be decided once it happens." However, the Taliban have said women will enjoy their rights in Afghanistan under the *Sharia* law. *Sharia* is the legal system of *Islam*. The Taliban have their own interpretation of *Sharia* law.[3]

Sharia, or Islamic law, influences the legal code in most Muslim countries. A movement to allow*sharia* to govern personal status law, a set of regulations that pertain to marriage, divorce, inheritance, and custody, is even expanding into the west. "There are so many varying interpretations of what *sharia* actually means that in some places, it can be incorporated into political system relatively easily," says CFR's Steven A. Cook. *Sharia's* influence on both personal status law and criminal law is highly controversial. Some interpretations are used to justify cruel punishments such as amputation and stoning, as well as unequal treatment of women in inheritance, dress, and independence. The debate is growing as to whether *sharia* can coexist with secularism, democracy, or even modernity, an idea that is being tested by several countries in the Middle East in the wake of popular uprisings and civil wars.[4]

While Terrorism – even in the form of suicide attacks – is not an Islamic phenomenon, it cannot be ignored that the lion's share of terrorist acts and the most devastating of them in recent years have been perpetrated in the name of *Islam*. This fact has sparked a fundamental debate both in the West and within the Muslim world regarding the link between these acts and the teachings of *Islam*. Most Western analysts are hesitant to identify such acts with the *Bonafede* teachings of one of the world's great religions and prefer to view them as a perversion of a religion that is essentially peace-loving and tolerant.[5]

As terrorism and violent extremism remain an increasingly high threat, there is a growing global consensus on the fact that military operations and security measures alone are not enough to defeat terrorism. In order to fully and efficiently respond to the challenges and threats that terrorism and violent extremism pose to nations, regions and communities today, greater emphasis should be put on prevention through reinforcing structural changes, community engagement, and building of resilience.Terrorist and violent extremist groups tend to largely take root in marginalized areas, using local grievances to recruit young citizens in vulnerable life situations, suffering for instance from varying degrees of unemployment, low education, and literacy levels. It is necessary to enhance effective governance addressing aggravating factors and underlying conditions that may create grievances and may lead individuals to join violent extremist groups.[6]

CHAPTER THREE

STATE OF ECONOMY AND DEVELOPMENT IN TALIBAN

The question of whether *Islam* affects economic performance is important for several reasons. Muslim-majority countries are appreciably poorer than the world's economically advanced countries, even the rest of the world. The average per capita income at purchasing power parity of the Fifty-seven-member Organisation of Islamic Cooperation was $10,015 in 2014; it was $17,500 for the world's remaining countries, and (excepting its 1 Muslim-majority member) $42,216 for the OECD, the club of economically advanced countries. Muslim-majority countries lag also in terms of other basic indices of economic performance, such as life expectancy and adult literacy. Within particular regions too, Muslim-majority countries lag behind those where Muslims are outnumbered. The Balkans, non-Arab Africa, and the Indian subcontinent offer cases in point. Yet, the world's poor countries include many that are overwhelmingly non-Muslim. That alone calls for care in attributing any economic outcome, whether favourable or unfavourable to religion. Another reason is that within multi-religious countries with a substantial Muslim share Muslims tend to be relatively poor. Moreover, this underperformance is observed regardless of whether Muslims are in the majority or minority. The world's Muslim-majority countries are spread across three continents, and substantial Muslim minorities exist in other parts of the world. Surely, the practice of *Islam* varies geographically, depending on local circumstances and influences. The promoters of the generalisations are certainly aware of the variations. They know, for instance, that the world's top-notch scientists include Muslims.[1]

A. **What are the Taliban's financial sources?**

1. **Opium, taxes, and extortion** – Afghanistan is the world's largest producer of opium. The Taliban earns money from taxes imposed at several stages of the process. A 10% cultivation tax is collected from opium farmers. Taxes are also collected from the laboratories converting opium into heroin, as well as the traders who smuggle the illicit drugs. The US military says 60% of Taliban funding comes from narcotics. By August 2018, the US claimed to have destroyed around two hundred of the estimated four hundred to five hundred Taliban drug laboratories in the country, nearly half of them in southern Helmand province. It was also claimed that the air campaign wiped out around a quarter of the Taliban's revenue from the opium trade. But the longer-term impact of this campaign is far from clear. Even when laboratories are destroyed, they are cheap and quick to rebuild.[2]

2. **Expanding areas of control** –It also draws revenue from businesses such as telecommunications and mobile phone operators. The head of Afghanistan's Electricity Company told the BBC earlier this year that the Taliban was earning more than $2m a year by billing electricity consumers in different parts of the country. There is also income generated directly from conflict. Each time the Taliban captures a military post or an urban centre, it empties treasuries and seizes scores of weapons, as well as cars and armoured vehicles.[3]

3. **Mines and minerals** – Most of the extraction is small scale and much of it is done illegally. The Taliban has taken control of mining sites and extorted money from ongoing legal and illegal mining operations. In its 2014 annual report, the UN Analytical Support and Sanctions Monitoring Team said the Taliban received more than the $10m a year from twenty-five to thirty illegal mining operations in southern Helmand province.[4]

As it is apparent that, the rule of law is only marginally functional, and the government and law enforcement did more to extort than support, a corrupt government and elite disguised the fact that real GDP per capita was some of the lowest in the world (ranking a low 213th out of two hundred and twenty-eight rated countries). Unemployment, and particularly youth unemployment, could not be measured accurately but were obviously critical problems. Public debt had reached one of the highest percentages of any country (202nd out of two hundred and twenty-eight). Drought and narcotrafficking were critical problems, large amounts of aid were wasted and stolen, and many claims of progress had no real justification.[5]

The Taliban may have governed in the past, but it was forced to seriously govern even at the local District levels for two decades. It has no cadres that have practical experience in dealing with these problems. No one can be sure what elements of the Taliban will take real power as it consolidates it rule, but all of these factors make it likely that it will quickly learn it needs outside trade and investment, a reasonable degree of international recognition, and substantial aid to deal with the challenges it faces at even a minimal level. Such an effort will have to be conditional on the Taliban being willing to compromise in some areas and its agreement to avoid links to active international terrorism. This may well prove to be impossible.[6]

According to a research report of Centre on International Cooperation (CIC), In the millions of words worth of Taliban publications and propaganda over the last decade, there has been precious little about the Taliban's view of the state. There appears to be no consensus on the shape of a future state, nor on the specifics of how it would function or administer territory, indicating that this has been grossly under-theorized within the movement. When speaking of an ideal state, some Talibanic people took for granted that it must be one based on *Sharia* law. This means, for them, that the state should be the primary guardian of faith and civil order for the benefit of its citizens. SN described it this way: "When we say Islamic state, it means the prime characteristic of such a state is to uphold *Islam*. With religious principles and parameters observed, such a state is responsible for ensuring public security and welfare of the citizens." 2 people provided a well-defined list of functions for such an ideal state: preserving, in order of importance, the religion, life, lineage (by prescribing marriage and forbidding extramarital relations), intellect (through education and through the prohibition of intoxicants that undermines one's intellectual ability, like alcohol and drugs), and property of its citizens. Indeed, these are the five foundational goals (*maqasid*) of *Sharia*. This means that safeguarding morals and preservation of civil order are sine qua non features of the Taliban state. Talibanic people rarely mentioned other possible state functions, such as safeguarding the rights of the individual (except property rights) or protecting social liberties and political freedoms.[7]

CHAPTER FOUR

SHARIA LAW: ISLAM, WOMEN, AND EXTREMISM

Sharia, widely known as the 'Islamic Law', is the Arabic word for 'the way' or 'the law'. Its origin in *Islam* is from four sources the *Quran*, the *Sunnah* and *Hadis* (words and text records of Prophet Muhammad), *Qiyas* (reasonable interpretation of the first two) and *Ijma* (consensus of jurists).[1] The *Hanbali* school, Islam's most orthodox, which spawned the *Wahhabi* and *Salafi* branches, is embraced in Saudi Arabia and by the Taliban. The *Hanafi* school, known for being the most liberal and the most focused on reason and analogy, is dominant among Sunnis in Central Asia, Egypt, Pakistan, India, China, Turkey, the Balkans, and the Caucasus. The *Maliki* school is dominant in North Africa and the *Sahafi* school in Indonesia, Malaysia, Brunei Darussalam, and Yemen. *Shia* Muslims follow the *Jafari* school, most notably in *Shia*-dominant Iran. The distinctions have more impact on the legal systems in each country, however, than on individual Muslims, as many do not adhere to one school in their personal lives.[2]

A. **Punishment and Equality Under Sharia: Extremism?[3]**

Marriage and divorce are the most significant aspects of *sharia*, while criminal law is the most controversial. In *Sharia*, there are categories of offences:[4] those that are prescribed a specific punishment in the *Quran*, known as *hadd* punishments, those that fall under a judge's discretion, and those resolved through a tit-for-tat measure (i.e., blood money paid to the family of a murder victim). There are five had crimes: unlawful sexual intercourse (sex outside of marriage and adultery), false accusation of unlawful sexual intercourse, wine drinking (sometimes extended to include all alcohol drinking), theft, and highway robbery. Punishments for *hadd* offences – flogging, stoning, amputation, exile, or execution – get a significant amount of media attention when they occur.

Extremist groups such as the al-*Qaeda* spinoff known as the Islamic State in Iraq and Syria (ISIS), have become notorious for executions by stoning and crucifixion. They apply *hadd* punishments rarely used in Islamic history. Vigilante justice also takes place. Honour killings, murders committed in retaliation for bringing dishonour on one's family, are a worldwide problem. While precise statistics are scarce, the UN estimates thousands of women are killed annually in the name of family honour. Other practices that are woven into the *sharia* debate, such as female genital cutting, child and adolescent marriages[5], polygamy, and gender-biased inheritance rules, elicit as much controversy.

Whether democracy and Islam can coexist is a topic of heated debate. Some conservative Muslims argue democracy is a purely Western concept imposed on Muslim countries. Others feel *Islam* necessitates a democratic system and that democracy has a basis in the *Quran* since 'mutual consultation' among the people is commended (42:38 *Quran*). Rather than rejecting democracy, many Muslims see *sharia* as a means "to be liberated from government corruption and believe it can exist within a democratic and inclusive framework." Some Muslim scholars say that secular government is the best way to observe *sharia*. "Enforcing a [*sharia*] through coercive power of the state negates its religious nature, because Muslims would be observing the law of the state and not freely performing their religious obligation as Muslims," says *sharia* expert Abdullahi Ahmed An-Na'im. [6]

B. Sharia for women –

In an article in The Conversation[7], Islamic Studies professor Asma Asfaruddin wrote that *Sharia* recognises "the absolute equality of men and women as human beings and proclaims that they are each other's partners in promoting the common good". According to Asfaruddin, *Sharia* "provides women with certain rights that were practically unheard of in the premodern world". These rights include education, divorce, abortion, and property inheritance. In May this year, Politics and Legal Studies professor Mark FathiMassoud wrote about how women in Somalia and Somaliland whom he interviewed were using Sharia to promote feminism. [8]

Saudi Arabia employs one of the strictest interpretations of *sharia*. Women are always under the guardianship of male relatives and must be completely covered in public. Elsewhere, governments are much more lenient, as in the United Arab Emirates, where alcohol is tolerated. Non-Muslims are not expected to obey *Sharia*, and in most countries, they are under the jurisdiction of special committees and adjunct courts under the control of the government.[9]

The problem with the Taliban's enforcement of the *Sharia* law lies in the extremely strict interpretation of the law as well as the harsh implementation. When the Taliban were in power in 1996-2001, this led to serious violations of the modern rights of equality and freedom of women, as well as violation of human rights of justice and trial as widely accepted in the modern world. Only a few countries at present allow for the *Hudud* punishments for crimes, which are Saudi Arabia, Iran, Brunei, Afghanistan, Indonesia, Sudan, Pakistan, Nigeria, and Qatar. *Sharia* is the basis of all Saudi law and until recently, it was common for extreme *Hudud* punishments to be carried out in public. The Saudi law has only recently allowed women to step out without a male chaperone and drive vehicles. Twenty years ago, the Taliban had imposed a very harsh interpretation of the *Sharia*, banning women form stepping out of the house, getting education, or working. They had banned music and appointed 'monitors' who would enforce these rules with violence.[10]

1. The Taliban have their own interpretation of Sharia law –*[11]*

Here's a brief to what the *Sharia* law means for women under the Taliban rule:

- Can women go out in the market? – They can. But during their previous rule, the Taliban made it conditional saying a woman needed to be accompanied by a male family member (child or adult) when she went out.
- Can women hang out with friends? – The Taliban had effectively placed women under house arrest in the past prohibiting them from hanging out with friends outside home.
- Can women meet male friends? – Women are not allowed to interact with boys over twelve or men who are not family.

- Can women get education? – Women can get education but not in a regular school, college, or madrasas where boys or men too study.
- Can women apply make-up? – During their previous rule, the Taliban had prohibited use of makeup including nail-polish by women.
- Can women play music and dance? – Music is illegal under *Sharia* law. The Taliban had punished those who had played music or danced on tunes at parties.
- Can women work in offices? – The Taliban have said women would be allowed to work. But reports from Afghanistan said bankers and employees of public offices were escorted by Taliban on their way home. They were told their male relatives could start working in their place.
- Is it mandatory to wear burqa? – Yes. Display of beauty is not allowed under *Sharia* law. The Taliban stipulate that girl above 8 must wear burqa when accompanying a male member of the family or when they interact with an outsider at home.
- How should women speak? – During the previous Taliban regime, it was prescribed that women should speak in a voice that is not audible to a stranger whether in a gathering of women or in public.
- Can women wear high heels? – Wearing high heeled shoes was banned by the Taliban, who stipulated that woman should walk in such a manner that no man should hear her footsteps.
- Can women sit on balconies? – Under the Taliban rule, women were not allowed to be seen on balconies of their homes.
- Can women do modelling of any kind? – Filming or displaying images of women anywhere including in newspapers, books, or posters was prohibited under the Taliban rule.
- What may happen if a woman breaks the *Sharia* law? –The Taliban carry out exemplary punishments for violation of the *Sharia* law. Women were, in the previous rule, sentenced to public humiliation, flogging, and stoning to death for different crimes under the *Sharia* law.[12]

In words of Alice Paul, "There will never be a new world order until women are a part of it". This may apply in the case of Taliban too.

CHAPTER FIVE

TERRORISM OR 'ISLAMIC TERRORISM'? – CAUSES AND RELIGIOUS SOURCES

Why are some societies more exposed to terrorism than others? What are the common theories and hypotheses concerning the causes of terrorism? A paper published by the Norwegian Defence Research Establishment surveyed theories on the causes of terrorism, as well as those for explaining terrorism on an international or world system level of analysis. Some theories in summarised form over the causes of terrorism was included:[1]

- Perceptions of deprivation and inequality, especially amongst culturally defined groups. This can lead to civil violence, of which terrorism may be a part. Terrorism represents social control from below, as attacks are directed upon targets symbolising central government or a superior community.
- A lack of political legitimacy and continuity, as well as a lack of integration for the political fringes, encourages ideological terrorism. The potential is exacerbated by ethnic diversity.
- Terrorism in one country can spill over into neighbouring areas. Mass media can influence the patterns of terrorism by enhancing agenda setting, increasing lethality, and expanding the transnational character.
- A skewed gender balance and high proportion of unmarried males increases the association with intra-societal violence and instability. Political and criminally motivated violence is largely the work of young unmarried men.
- Windows of opportunity when terrorist violence can serve to influence opinion and resource. In the case of peace agreements, radical members

of coalition groups resume and escalate hostilities to undermine confidence and prevent compromise, thus regaining the initiative and avoiding marginalisation.

- Hegemony in the international system by one or two actors will cause a high level of transnational anti-systematic terrorism as a war by proxy develops. Therefore, terrorism can represent a backlash against globalisation and modernisation.

Terrorism can occur in a variety of manners and instances. Terrorists may be deprived, uneducated, affluent and from both sexes. It can occur in developed and undeveloped countries, in a variety of regimes. It encompasses ideology and religion. Though what gives rise to terrorism may be different from what perpetuates terrorism over time. Societies that are more exposed tend to be:[2]

- Poor societies with weak state structures. These are more exposed to civil wars than wealthier countries, and therefore the risk of terrorism increases.
- States engaged in democratic transition rather than democratic or authoritarian regimes. Levels of transnational terrorism[3] are highest in semi-authoritarian states.
- Undergoing societal changes brought through modernisation. Thus, creating the conditions for terrorism through mobility, communication, widespread targets and audiences.
- Weak and collapsed states that contribute to international terrorism. Ongoing or past wars can have terrorism motivations rooted within. Armed conflicts also have facilitating influences on transnational terrorism.

A. **Links between *Islam* and violent extremism –**

It is far too easy for analysts who are not Muslim to focus on the small part of the extremist threat that Muslim extremists pose to non-Muslims in the West and/or demonise one of the world's great religions, and to drift into some form of Islamophobia – blaming a faith for patterns of violence that are driven by a tiny fraction of the world's Muslims and by many other factors like population, failed governance, and weak economic development. It is equally easy to avoid analysing the links between extremist violence and Islam in order to be politically correct or to avoid provoking Muslims and the governments of largely Muslim states. The end result is to ignore the reality that most extremist and terrorist violence does occur in largely Muslim states, although it overwhelmingly consists of attacks by Muslim extremists on fellow Muslims, and not some clash between civilisations.[4]

If one examines a wide range of sources, however, a number of key patterns emerge that make five things very clear:[5]

- First, most extremist and violent terrorist incidents do occur in largely Muslim states.
- Second, most of these incidents are perpetrated by a small minority of Muslims seeking power primarily in their own areas of operation and whose primary victims are fellow Muslims.
- Third, almost all of the governments of the countries involved are actively fighting extremism and terrorism, and most are allies of Western states that work closely with the security, military, and counterterrorism forces of non-Muslim states to fight extremism and terrorism.
- Fourth, the vast majority of Muslims oppose violent extremism and terrorism, and,
- Fifth, religion is only one of many factors that lead to instability and violence in largely Muslim states. It is a critical ideological force in shaping the current patterns of extremism, but it does not represent the core values of Islam and many other far more material factors help lead to the rise of extremism.

B. **Global patterns of Terrorism are dominated by Extremism in largely Muslim states –[6]**

The previous section makes it clear that the patterns of extremist violence are dominated by violence in largely Muslim states and by extremist movements that claim to represent Islamic values. It is important to note, that only a relatively small portion of the incidents can be attributed to ISIS (Islamic State of Iraq and Syiria)[7], even using the highest START estimate.[8] More broadly, even if Afghanistan is added to the total for Iraq and Syria, the three major countries where the U.S. and other outside states partner with Muslim governments accounted for 26,113 incidents – or only 37% of the global total. Moreover, even if one counts all of the MENA region and South Asia, key organised extremist groups like Al Qaeda, Al Nusra, ISIS, and the Taliban[9] accounted for 12,159 incidents or 17% of the total. Defeating today's key perpetrators is critical, but it in no way will defeat the longer-term threat.[10]

Modern International Islamist terrorism is a natural offshoot of twentieth-century Islamic fundamentalism. The 'Islamic Movement' emerged in the Arab world and British ruled India as a response to the dismal state of Muslim society in those countries: social injustice, rejection of traditional mores, acceptance of foreign domination and culture. It perceives the malaise of modern Muslim societies as having strayed from the 'straight path' (*as-sirat al-mustaqim*) and the solution to all ills in a return to the original mores of *Islam*. The problems addressed may be social or political: inequality, corruption, and oppression. But in traditional *Islam* – and certainly in the worldview of the Islamic fundamentalist – there is no separation between the political and the religious. *Islam* is, in essence, both religion and regime (*din wa-dawla*) and no area of human activity is outside its remit. Be the nature of the problems as it may, "*Islam* is the solution."[11]

C. Jihad –[12]

Until the 1980s, attempts to mobilize Muslims all over the world for a *jihad* in one area of the world (Palestine, Kashmir) were unsuccessful. The Soviet invasion of Afghanistan was a watershed event, as it revived the concept of participation in *Jihad* to evict an 'infidel' occupier from a Muslim country as a 'personal duty' (lard'ein) for every capable Muslims and for Muslim territories. Therefore, any land (Afghanistan, Palestine, Kashmir, Chechnya, Spain) that had once been under the sway of Islamic law may not revert to control by any other law. In such a case, it becomes the 'personal duty' of all Muslims in the land to fight a *jihad* to liberate it. If they fail, it becomes incumbent on any Muslim in a certain perimeter from that land to join the *jihad* and so forth. Accordingly, given the number of Muslim lands under 'infidel occupation' and the length of time of those occupations, it is argued that it has become a personal duty for all Muslims to join the *jihad*. This duty – if taken seriously – is no less a religious imperative than the other five pillars of *Islam* (the statement of belief or *Shahadah*, prayer, fasting, charity, and *haj*). It becomes a *defacto* (and in the eyes of some a *dejure*) sixth pillar; a Muslim who does not perform it will inherit hell. Such a philosophy attributing centrality to the duty of *jihad* is not an innovation of modern radical *Islam*.

An offshoot of this philosophy poses a dilemma for theories of deterrence. The Islamic traditions of war allow the Muslims forces to retreat if their numerical strength is less than half that of the enemy. Other traditions go further and allow retreat only in the face of a tenfold superiority of the enemy. The reasoning is that the act of *jihad* is, by definition, an act of faith in *Allah*. By fighting a weaker or equal enemy, the Muslim is relying on his own strength and not on *Allah*; by entering the fray against all odds, the *mujahid[13]* is proving his utter faith in *Allah* and will be rewarded accordingly. The politics of Islamist radicalism has also bred a mentality of hello ergo sum (I fight; therefore, I exist) – Islamic leaders are in constant need of popular jihads to boost their leadership status.[14]

D. Western Dilemma –

It is a tendency in politically oriented Western society to assume that there is a rational pragmatic cause for act of terrorism and that if the political grievance is addressed properly, the phenomenon will fade. However, when the roots are not political, it is naïve to expect political gestures to change the hearts of radicals. Attempts to deal with the terrorist threat as if it were divorced from its intellectual, cultural, and religious sources are doomed to failure. Counterterrorism begins on the religious-ideological level and must adopt appropriate methods. The cultural and religious sources of radical Islamic ideology must be addressed in order to develop a long-range strategy for coping with the terrorist threat to which they give birth.[15]

Terrorist and violent extremist groups tend to largely take root in marginalized areas, using local grievances to recruit young citizens as vulnerable life situations, suffering for instance form varying degrees of unemployment, low education and literacy levels. It is necessary to enhance effective governance addressing aggravating factors and underlying conditions that may create grievances and may lead individuals to join violent extremist groups. Women of all ages are increasingly becoming a target of extremist violence and terrorist acts, including the uses of sexual violence and slavery to undermine their essential freedoms and rights. Terrorist groups also leverage on traditional gender norms and dynamics within certain societies to enforce violence and perpetuate extremist acts.[16]

CHAPTER SIX

CONCLUSION

Only by setting up a clear demarcation between orthodox and radical *Islam* can the radical elements be exorcised. The priority of solidarity within the Islamic world plays into the hands of the radicals. Only an Islamic *Kulturkampf*[1] can redraw the boundaries between radical and moderate in favour of the latter. Such a struggle must be based on an in-depth understanding of the religious sources for justification of Islamist terrorism and a plan for the creation of a legitimate moderate counterbalance to the radical narrative in *Islam*. A strategy to cope with radical Islamic ideology cannot take shape without a reinterpretation of Western concepts of the boundaries of the freedoms of religion and speech, definitions of religious incitement, and criminal culpability of religious leaders for the acts of their flock because of their spiritual influence. Such a reinterpretation impinges on basic principles of Western civilisation and law. Under the circumstances, it is the lesser evil.[2]

In the words of Ali Gomaa[3], grand mufti of Egypt, "One of the most important contributions made by the Western world to the global culture is the concept of modernity itself. As has often been noted, modernity is not simply a particular epoch in the history of the world, but also a set of very large and important structural and material changes affecting people globally...... In particular, we have the new concept of 'alternative modernity', a term which goes a long way in representing the diversity of the world in encountering new realities. So, whereas it was previously thought that to be modern meant to distance oneself from religion and tradition, it is becoming evident that, throughout the centuries, community leaders have found innovative and creative ways to relate religion and tradition to new advances in technology, politics, and economics and so as to provide pragmatic guidance in an ever-changing world. That is to say, it was, and is, possible to remain authentic to one's religious traditions while still being a modern person. From the Muslim viewpoint, these commitments must be recognised by all involved, if we are to engage in a truly fruitful dialogue".[4]

Threats form violent extremism and terrorism have increased in recent years and have become more and more interlinked at local, regional, and international levels. Violent extremism and terrorism are exacerbating existing governance and inequality challenges within countries and societies and increasing the risk of violent conflict. Violent extremist groups exploit and reinforce divisions among social groups and undermine the social contract between citizens and their governments. Women of all ages are increasingly becoming a target of extremist violence and terrorist acts, including the use of sexual violence and slavery to undermine their essential freedoms and rights. Terrorist groups also leverage on traditional gender norms and dynamics within certain societies to enforce violence and perpetuate extremist acts. To deal with this to some extent, UN Women's strategic plan 2018-2021[5] outlined continued work and contribution to the prevention of violent extremism.[6]

If we consider religious sources as one reason for terrorism, then the radical narrative, which promises paradise to those who perpetrate acts of terrorism, must be met by an equally legitimate religious force which guarantees hellfire for the same acts. Some elements of such rulings should be, inter alia:[7]

- A call for renewal of *ijtihad[8]* as the basis to reform Islamic dogmas and to relegate old dogmas to historic contexts.
- That there exists no state of *jihad* between *Islam* and the rest of the world (hence, *jihad* is not a personal duty).
- That the violation of the physical safety of a non-Muslim in a Muslim country is prohibited (*haram*).
- That suicide bombings are clear acts of suicide, and therefore, their perpetrators are condemned to eternal hellfire.
- That moral or financial support of acts of terrorism is also *haram*. [9]
- That a legal ruling claiming *jihad* is a duty derived from the root of *Islam* is a falsification of the roots of *Islam*, and therefore, those who make such statements have performed acts of heresy.

Again, in the words of grand mufti,[10]

...... In fact, these radical attitudes stand as an offence to the humane tradition of learning that characterises Islamic history. Instead of seeking to create havoc and chaos in the world, Islam facilitates the application of the wisdom and moral strength of religion in changing and uncertain times. It is through adopting this approach that an authentic, contemporary, moderate, and tolerant Islam can provide solutions to the problems confronting the Muslim world today. One of the problems faced by religious communities today is the issue of authority. In both Islam and other religions, we are witnessing a phenomenon in which lay people without a sound foundation in religious learning have attempted to set themselves up as religious authorities, even though they lack the scholarly qualifications for making valis interpretations of religious law and morality. It is this eccentric and rebellious attitude towards religion that opens the way for extremist interpretations of Islam that have no basis in reality. Furthermore, and this must be stressed, none of these extremists have been educated in Islam in genuine centres of Islamic learning. They are, rather, products of troubled environments and have subscribed to distorted and misguided interpretations of Islam that have no basis in traditional Islamic doctrine. Their aim is purely political and has no religious foundation. It is to create havoc and chaos in the world.[11]

Following a religion and blind faith towards an orthodox and radical religious rules are two separate ideas. A nation with such obsolete approach cannot exist in future, it lacks in its economic and overall development which ultimately makes the inhabitants discontented as they feel dodged and unable to keep pace with other economies and civilisations which leads to crimes, stunned humanity and ultimately finding escape by crushingthe true form of religion through delusions to justify acts like terrorism. The extremism is a bigger threat to the world than any religion.